FAITH TALK

WORD OF GOD SPEAK
A 90 Day Devotional to Grow Your Faith

FAITH TALK
Copyright © 2019 by Vondalee Chipman.

Published by Hope for the Home, Inc.
6933 Commons Plaza, Suite 242
Chesterfield, VA 23832
Printed in the United States of America

FAITH TALK

WORD OF GOD SPEAK
A 90 Day Devotional to Grow Your Faith

VONDA CHIPMAN

TABLE OF CONTENTS

DEDICATION

I dedicate this book to my loving husband, Dr. Paul Chipman, who has been a constant inspiration and example for me to pursue becoming an author.

ACKNOWLEDGEMENTS

My foremost acknowledgement of thanksgiving is to Jesus Christ, my Savior, my Lord, and the author and finisher of my faith. Without Him depositing His faith in me, I would have had nothing to write or share. To my husband, sons, and everyone who prayed for me and helped me to complete this book, I express my heartfelt appreciation to all of you.

INTRODUCTION

My purpose for writing this devotional is to inspire you to develop a hunger and thirst for what lies beyond the veil that separates the natural world from the spiritual. There exists an unseen dimension that is governed and activated by an invisible spiritual force called faith. By the sheer energy of your faith, you can go where no one has gone. You can do what no one has done. By faith, you can see and possess all that God has in store for you in the spiritual realm of His kingdom. With your voice, you can release powerful words of faith to call forth from heaven to earth the blessings of God reserved just for you.

I believe that as you meditate on the daily Faith Talks and apply the Faith Action Steps, your faith will catapult your mind to capture the profound truth of your limitless power. From this moment forward, I believe you will live your life supernaturally from the kingdom of heaven. Thus, it is my prayer that you will grasp the profundity of the Scripture, "we are in the world but not of the world" (John 17:11,14,16). Let the one who has eyes to see, see and ears to hear, hear.

MONTH 1

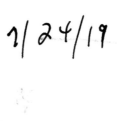

7/24/19

DAY 1

God Is Speaking
Are You Listening?

"God Who at various times and in various ways spoke in times past to the fathers by the prophets, has in these last days spoken to us by His Son, Whom also He has appointed heir of all things, through Whom also He made the worlds." Hebrews 1:1-2

God is always speaking. He speaks through Jesus, His Son. He speaks through creation. He speaks through the Scriptures. He speaks through His Holy Spirit. He speaks in dreams and visions. He speaks through people. He speaks through parents, apostles, prophets, pastors, priests, teachers, and evangelists. He even speaks through babies and children. God is speaking to you!

Jesus said, "My sheep hear My voice, and I know them, and they follow Me." John 10:27

<u>Faith Action Step</u>

Be still and listen for His voice. Then reply, Yes Lord, I am listening. What do you want me to do?

7/24/19

Wait on The Lord

DAY 2

Ears to Hear

"He who has an ear, let him hear
what the Spirit says to the churches." Revelation 2:7

Y ou have natural ears to hear natural sounds and words. You will also need spiritual ears to hear spiritual sounds and words. God is Spirit. He speaks spiritual words. Open your spirit to hear and receive His words.

"It is the Spirit that gives life; the flesh profits nothing. The words
that I speak to you are spirit, and they are life." John 6:63

Faith Action Step

Pray for spiritual ears to hear. Ask Holy Spirit to give you the ability to hear and understand God's spiritual words.

7/24/19

DAY 3

Eyes to See

"For we walk by faith and not by sight." 2 Corinthians 5:7

Just as people have eyes to see material objects in the material world, people also possess spiritual eyes to see spiritual objects in the spiritual world. With our spiritual eyes, we see God and see as God sees. Only with the spiritual eyes of faith will people be able to see into the spiritual realm those things that are impossible to see in the natural realm. Faith is spiritual not material. Faith perceives as an undeniable truth those things that are not ascertained by the natural senses. With our eyes of faith, we can see and possess spiritual riches in the spirit realm. We can command unseen things to manifest in the natural world.

"Now faith is the substance of things hoped for,
the evidence of things not seen." Hebrews 11:1

Faith Action Step

Decide right now that you will live your life by your spiritual eyes of faith. Commit to praying for Holy Spirit to give you 20/20 spiritual vision to see as God sees.

DAY 4

Live What You Truly Believe

"But the just shall live by his faith." Habakkuk 2:4

If you have faith in God, then live by the faith of God. The faith of God sees what is before *it is*. It knows for certain *it is* will be because God said, *"It is so"*. God has faith in His own words to produce what He thinks and says. God gave you the same measure of faith as Jesus. The fruit of the Spirit is faith. You have the same Spirit of faith as Jesus. He expects you to use it.

"... Believe in the Lord your God, and you shall be established; believe His prophets, and you shall prosper." II Chronicles 20:20

Faith Action Step

Use the faith of Jesus in you to believe, receive, and call forth the promises of God to you.

7/24/19

DAY 5

Enjoy Trusting God

"Oh, taste and see that the Lord is good;
Blessed is the man who trusts in Him!" Psalms 34:8 I

It is so sweet to trust in Jesus! God wants you to enjoy trusting and depending upon Him. The hymnal lyrics of Elisha A. Hoffman and Anthony J. Showalter, "What a fellowship, what a joy divine, leaning on the everlasting arms; What a blessedness, what a peace is mine, leaning on the everlasting arms" depict the beauty and blessed joy of trusting God. Divine trust creates happiness in God and you. Make God happy by developing a confident trust in Him!

"And without trusting, it is impossible to be well pleasing to God,
because whoever approaches him must trust that He does exist and
that He becomes a Rewarder to those who seek him out."
Hebrews 11:6 (CJB)

Faith Action Step
Make up your mind to trust God and enjoy trusting Him.

DAY 6

Can God Trust You to Trust Him?

"Trust in Him at all times, you people; Pour out your heart before Him; God is a refuge for us." Psalms 62:8

My husband, Dr. Paul Chipman, often says, "If you can't see God's hand, you can always trust His heart. We walk by faith and not by sight." Just because you are unable to see the hand of God working for you, don't assume that He is not working. Just because you don't hear from God, don't assume that He is not listening. God is always working and listening. During times of testing, the teacher is silent. The student must trust that she knows what the teacher has taught her. She must trust that she is prepared and ready to pass the test. Can God trust you to trust Him without worrying?

"And shall God not avenge His own elect who cry out day and night to Him, though He bears long with them? I tell you that He will avenge them speedily. Nevertheless, when the Son of Man comes, will He really find faith on the earth?" Luke 18:7-8

Faith Action Step

Trust God and believe that you have the faith to pass the tests that come your way. Believe that you are ready and prepared for promotion to the next level of faith.

DAY 7

Live by the Spirit of Faith

"And since we have the same spirit of faith, according to what is written, "I believed and therefore I spoke," we also believe and therefore speak," II Corinthians 4:13

The Spirit of faith is the spirit of trust, endurance, and excellence. Live by the Spirit of faith in dependence on God's Word. Keep believing and speaking His Word until it manifests what you believe.

"If you abide in Me, and My words abide in you, you will ask what you desire, and it shall be done for you." John 15:7

Faith Action Step

Read the Gospel of John Chapters 14 and 15. Latch onto a promise of Jesus from one of those chapters. Hold fast onto it with bulldog faith without letting go. Keep declaring and doing what it says to do until the promise manifests in your life.

DAY 8

God Will Provide

"Do not remember the former things, nor consider the things of old. Behold, I will do a new thing, now it shall spring forth; Shall you not know it? I will even make a road in the wilderness and rivers in the desert." Isaiah 43:18-19

Trust God to provide in a new way. He likes to surprise us. He never wants us to think He is predictable. Yes, God is faithful. Yet, He is not monotonous. God provided food for the Prophet Elijah, by an extremely unorthodox way. In the time of the three-year drought and famine which Elijah called forth, God commanded him to hide by a brook and drink water from it. God also commanded the ravens to bring bread and meat to Elijah twice a day. Yes, you read correctly. Ravens fed Elijah. Go ravens!!

Later, the brook dried because God had an unanticipated plan of provision for Elijah. He wanted to bless a widow who happened to live in the home country of Elijah's archenemy, Queen Jezebel. Jezebel was seeking to kill him. Her father was the king of Sidon.

God sent Elijah to enemy territory for a most unlikely person to feed him, an impoverished single parent widow. His faith in God was strong enough to trust and obey God even if it meant absolute nonsense to him. Elijah went to Zarephath to bless and be blessed. Because of Elijah's and the widow's obedience to God, she and her son had an abundance of food and water until Elijah ended the drought. Can God send you into the enemy's territory to bless and be blessed if He chooses?

"Then the word of the Lord came to him, saying,
"Arise, go to Zarephath, which belongs to Sidon and dwell there.
See, I have commanded a widow there to provide for you.
So he arose and went to Zarephath." 1 Kings 17:8-10

Faith Action Step

Give God your trust. Permit Him to provide for you according to His good and perfect will. Declare to God your commitment to allow Him to bless You as He pleases.

DAY 9

Faith to Give

"Do not lay up for yourselves treasures on earth, where moth and rust destroy and where thieves break in and steal; but lay up for yourselves treasures in heaven, where neither moth nor rust destroys and where thieves do not break in and steal. For where your treasure is, there your heart will be also." Matthew 6:19-21

God has a better way for you to live and get your needs met. It's the live to give way of life. When we live to give to God first, to finance and advance His kingdom in the earth, He will supernaturally multiply us with more to give. Of the increase of His government there is no end. Your kingdom of God financial investments are secure, fail proof, and theft proof. Kingdom people live to give and let God increase them. It is impossible to run out or run short of anything that God's abundant kingdom can supply.

People who depend on the world's economic system work to pay bills and increase themselves. When world system people lose their jobs, they lose their peace. Kingdom people's peace comes from trusting God to provide. Therefore, they can lose their jobs without losing their peace.

"Give and it will be given to you: good measure, pressed down, shaken, together, and running over will be put into your bosom." Luke 6:38

Faith Action Step

Live to give. Resist the spirit of fear. Trust God to provide for you abundantly.

DAY 10

As They Went Faith

"And they lifted up their voices and said, "Jesus, Master, have mercy on us!" So when He saw them, He said to them, "Go, show yourselves to the priests." And so it was that as they went, they were cleansed."
Luke 17:13-14

Sometimes the only instruction that you will hear from Jesus is "go". You will have to take it by faith that as you go the blessing will show. Stop looking for a sign first. Stop wanting to understand the Lord's command before you decide to obey it. Delayed obedience is disobedience. *As they went faith* is the type of faith that totally trusts in the Word of God and obeys the Word without requiring scientific evidence, human reasoning, or natural senses to confirm it.

Now the Lord said to Abram: "Get out of your country, from your family and from your father's house to a land that I will show you."
Genesis 12:1

Faith Action Step

Develop a strong trust in Jesus. Devote time daily to reflect and thank God for the many blessings and trials He has helped you to overcome. Meditate on His faithfulness and trustworthiness to you in the past. Expect Him to continue to help you to overcome today, tomorrow, and forever.

DAY 11

What Kind of Faith Do You Have?

He responded, "Have the kind of trust that comes from God!"
Mark 11:22 CJB

Some people trust and depend on their intellect, education, money, and relationships to advance in life. However, human faith is conjured from human strength rather than confidence in God. This is not the kind of trust that comes from God. The God kind of faith is the kind of trust that depends on God, only.

"Lean on, trust in, and be confident in the Lord with all your heart and mind and do not rely on your own insight or understanding."
Proverbs 3:5 AMPC

<u>Faith Action Step</u>
Trust God completely. Ask the Holy Spirit to reveal areas of your life where you are trusting in money, people, or things instead of God.

DAY 12

Faith, Patience, and Obedience Are Treasures in the Kingdom of God

"And we desire that each one of you show the same diligence to the full assurance of hope until the end, that you do not become sluggish, but imitate those who through faith and patience inherit the promises." Hebrews 6:11-12

Faith is trusting God completely. When you add to your faith, patience, which is long suffering and endurance, you accrue much compounded spiritual interest in your individual righteousness account (IRA). Faithful obedience to God with a sincere heart as a lifestyle will assure you the highest dividends and heavenly rewards available.

"If they obey and serve Him, they shall spend their days in prosperity, And their years in pleasures." Job 36:11

Faith Action Step

Desire to please Jesus with faith and obedience to His Word. Ask Holy Spirit to give you a hunger and thirst for God. Trust Him to empower you to love and obey God's Word completely.

DAY 13

Speak Faith Words

"For out of the abundance of the heart, the mouth speaks."
Matthew 12:34

What is in your heart will come out of your mouth. If you think lack and failure, you will speak lack and failure. If you think prosperity and good success, you will speak prosperity and good success. You will have what you say.

"Keep your heart with all diligence,
for out of it spring the issues of life." Proverbs 4:23

Faith Action Step

Pay attention to what you are saying. Commit to hiding the Word of God in your heart. You will soon begin to speak God's words more than your words. Read Psalm 119 regularly.

DAY 14

Believe It Today
Receive It Today

"And whatever things you ask in prayer, believing you will receive."
Matthew 21:22

Your prayer of faith sets in motion an immediate chain of events in heavenly places. As soon as you utter a prayer of faith, angels suddenly ascend and descend from heaven to earth to bring you the answer. Jesus told Nathanael that the heavens will open, and he will see angels ascending and descending from heaven on the Son of Man (John 1:51).

"Don't you realize that I could ask My Father for
thousands of angels to protect us, and he would send them instantly?"
Matthew 26:53 NLT

Faith Action Step

Meditate on a promise of Scripture that you desire to manifest in your life. Now see yourself as already having it. When you pray that Scripture for the first time, receive it by faith when you pray. From that moment forward, give God praise and thanksgiving daily for the answered prayer. He released it when you received it by faith. It's on the way, now. Keep praising God for it until it fully manifests.

DAY 15

Don't Pull Up Your Faith Seed

"But let him ask in faith, with no doubting, for he who doubts is like a wave of the sea driven and tossed by the wind. For let not that man suppose that he will receive anything from the Lord." James 1:6-7

The Word of God is an incorruptible seed. Plant it in your heart. Speak it with your mouth. It will always do what you send it to do if you plant it in faith. If you allow doubt and unbelief to contaminate your seeds, then you are bound to receive a harvest of weeds.

"Have faith in God," Jesus answered. "Truly, I tell you, if anyone says to this mountain, 'Go, throw yourself into the sea,' and does not doubt in their heart but believes that what they say will happen, it will be done for them." Mark 11:21-23 NIV

Faith Action Step

Remember and reflect upon the things that you may have stopped believing God to do for you. Repent of doubt and unbelief. Renew your faith for them, now. Apply Mark 11:21-23.

DAY 16

See Yourself as God Sees You

"Can a woman forget her nursing child, and not have compassion on the son of her womb? Surely, they may forget, Yet I will not forget you. See, I have inscribed you on the palm of My hands;"
Isaiah 49:15-16

Forget about the regrets of the past. Forget about the negative things that people have thought or said about you. Forget about the negative thoughts and feelings that you may have felt about yourself. Forget about the condemnation that others may have spoken against you. See yourself as God sees you. God sees you whole instead of broken. God sees you blessed and highly favored instead of guilty and condemned. God sees you worthy instead of worthless. God is love. He always thinks good thoughts towards you. He always wants to bless you. Read the Bible for yourself to discover how much God truly loves you.

"For I know the thoughts that I think toward you, says the Lord, thoughts of peace and not of evil, to give you a future and a hope."
Jeremiah 29:11

Faith Action Step

Build your trust in God's love for you. Each morning and night look into the mirror and tell yourself, "God says, I am good. He has good plans for me. He will not forget me!"

DAY 17

Take off the Weight

"Therefore, we also, since we are surrounded by so great a cloud of witnesses, let us lay aside every weight, and the sin which so easily ensnares us, and let us run with endurance the race that is set before us, looking unto Jesus, the author and finisher of our faith, who for the joy that was set before Him endured the cross, despising the shame, and has sat down at the right hand of the throne of God."
Hebrews 12:1-2

Shame is a weight.
Anger is a weight.
Discouragement is a weight
Weights cause depression. Remove the weights. Refuse to live a **S.A.D.** life.

"Anxiety in the heart of man causes depression, but a good word makes it glad." Proverbs 12:25

Faith Action Step

Write on a piece of paper the top three things that worry you. Tell them to Jesus. Tear the paper into small pieces. Now, as you throw them into the trash, say, "Jesus, I am giving these worries to you. I will let you take them and keep them. I will not take them back. You can have them forever." Thank You, Jesus.

DAY 18

Don't Quit

"I can do all things through Christ who strengthens me."
Philippians 4:13

Winners never quit. Quitters never win. You are a winner. You were born to win. Winners always win.

"But thanks be to God, who gives us the victory through our Lord Jesus Christ. Therefore, my brethren, be steadfast, immovable, always abounding in the work of the Lord, knowing that your labor is not in vain in the Lord." 1 Corinthians 15:58

Faith Action Step
Decide today that quitting is not an option.

DAY 19

Yield Not to Temptation

"No temptation has overtaken you except such as is common to man; but God is faithful, who will not allow you to be tempted beyond what you are able, but with the temptation will also make the way of escape, that you may be able to bear it." I Corinthians 10:13

Y ou are not alone. You have help. You have a Friend. Oh, what a friend you have in Jesus! You can resist the power of sin. Simply, ask Jesus to help you. The Lord knows how to deliver the godly out of temptations (2 Peter 2:9). Let God help you!

"And do not lead us into temptation But deliver us from the evil one. For Yours is the kingdom and the power and the glory forever. Amen." Matthew 6:13

Faith Action Step

When you are tempted to give into temptation, resist it and pray. Ask Holy Spirit to show you the way of escape, then immediately take it.

DAY 20

Control Your Soul

"By your patience possess your souls." Luke 21:19

Shut the door on impatience. It will only get you into trouble. God moves at His own pace. Give Him time to work things out, regardless of how long it takes. You just need to wait.

"Rest in the Lord and wait patiently for Him. But those who wait on the Lord, they shall inherit the earth." Psalms 37:7, 9

Faith Action Step

Learn to wait on God. Trust that God knows what He is doing. Accept and appreciate His timing.

DAY 21

Good Things Come to Those Who Wait

"Wait on the Lord. Be of good courage. Wait I say on the Lord."
Psalm 27:13

Waiting can feel uncomfortable. Yet, patience brings much reward. Waiting is much like baking. It is a process that requires ample time to complete. The process of baking a cake illustrates the motto of our United States of America, E pluribus unum, *out of many one*. In baking a cake, all the ingredients combine to make one delicious cake. Consuming cake ingredients individually may be unpleasant to your palate. Eating a raw egg or a half teaspoon of baking powder tastes and feels awful in your mouth. However, combined with the other ingredients, milk, butter, sugar, flour, and cocoa, the raw eggs and baking powder blend in well. The aroma of the mixture smells and tastes delicious. Yet, the cake mixture is not the cake.

In the crucible of the hot oven, the concoction is transformed into a beautiful delicious chocolate cake. It must remain in that fiery trial for a protracted period until it is completely done and ready to be served. Even after the cake is completely cooked, there is more waiting. A cooling period before eating ensures that the cake will not fall apart or cause injury by burning the mouths of the those who will eat it.

Similarly, our lives are akin to the baking process. Though our fiery trials may seem like unnecessary hardships, they are preparing and purifying us for the Master's service to God and humanity. Be patient. Trust the process. Remember, impatience often causes injury. Only God knows when you have been fully perfected and completed. Trust His omniscience. He alone knows when you are truly ready to come out of the fire. After all, God has very little use for half-baked Christians.

"Therefore the Lord will wait, that He may be gracious to you; And therefore He will be exalted, that He may have mercy on you. For the Lord is a God of justice. Blessed are all those who wait for Him."
Isaiah 30:18

Faith Action Step

Believe that God is working in you and around you to bless you.

DAY 22

Jesus Is with You

*"Jesus said, "...lo, I am with you always,
even to the end of the age." Amen." Matthew 28:20*

E motional reasoning is believing something is true because you feel as though it is true. Just because you feel alone doesn't mean you are alone. Jesus is with you. Act like you know He is present.

*"For He Himself has said, "I will never leave you nor forsake you."
So we may boldly say: "The Lord is my helper; I will not fear.
What can man do to me?" Hebrews 13:5-6*

Faith Action Step

Talk to Jesus. Ask Him to converse with you. Jesus is knocking at the door of your heart. Invite Him in to fellowship with you (Revelation 3:20).

DAY 23

Let God Avenge You

"Bless those who persecute you; bless and do not curse. Rejoice with those who rejoice, and weep with those who weep. Repay no one evil for evil. Have regard for good things in the sight of all men. If it is possible, as much as depends on you, live peaceably with all men. Beloved, do not avenge yourselves, but rather give place to wrath; for it is written, "Vengeance is Mine, I will repay," says the Lord. Do not be overcome by evil but overcome evil with good."
Romans 12:14-15, 17-19, 21

People are people. God is God. Only God is without sin. Therefore, all people, (including you and I) have sinned against God and other people. Knowing the truth about us, our heavenly Father foreordained a plan to repay us with goodness and blessings for the wrongs we suffer from others and the wrongs others have suffered from us. There is a purpose to your pain. Your suffering has value. If you suffer wrongly for justice and faithfulness to God, you have a promise of a great reward. El Roi (The God Who sees me), will surely reward you.

"Blessed are you when they revile and persecute you and say all kinds of evil against you falsely for My sake. Rejoice and be exceedingly glad, for great is your reward in heaven, for so they persecuted the prophets who were before you." Matthew 5:11-12

Faith Action Step

When you feel as though others have treated you unjustly, remember how you have mistreated others also. Forgive others as Jesus Christ has forgiven you for your sins. Pray for your offenders to grow in the grace and love of Jesus.

DAY 24

Love Is Sacrificial

"I have been crucified with Christ; it is no longer I who live, but Christ lives in me; and the life which I now live in the flesh I live by faith in the Son of God, who loved me and gave Himself for me."
Galatians 2:20

God is love. Love sacrifices. To become a sacrifice, someone or something living must die for others to live. Jesus sacrificed His life to give you spiritual life. Likewise, God commands you to be spiritually crucified with Christ and to sacrifice your life, will, ambition, and dreams to Jesus. Jesus Christ is God. God is love.

"By this we know love, because He laid down His life for us. And we also ought to lay down our lives for the brethren."
I John 3:16

Faith Action Step

Ask Holy Spirit, the Spirit of Truth, to reveal to you what you need to sacrifice to Jesus today.

DAY 25

Accept God's Love

'The Lord has appeared of old to me, saying':
"Yes, I have loved you with an everlasting love; Therefore,
with lovingkindness I have drawn you." Jeremiah 31:3

L ove is a gift. Gifts are given. God's love is His gift to you. God loves to give of Himself freely to all who will receive Him. If you are seeking to earn God's love, then you will become very disappointed. God's love is unmerited. How can you earn what is freely given?

No matter how hard you try, it is impossible to earn love. To earn means to receive a payment for labor. Earning is a business transaction. Love that is earned is counterfeit. It is control disguising as love. True love is given freely and unconditionally. Your unmerited love for others is evidence of your faith in God's love for you.

"Greater love has no one than this, than to lay down one's life
for his friends. You are My friends if you do whatever I command you.
As the Father loved Me, I also have loved you; abide in My love."
John 15:13, 14, 9

<u>Faith Action Step</u>
Freely receive God's unconditional love. Accept God's love for you based on His character and not yours. God is love. Love God because He is God. Love God unconditionally because He first loved you unconditionally.

DAY 26

Love Hurts

"You have heard that it was said,' You shall love your neighbor and hate your enemy.' But I say to you, love your enemies, bless those who curse you, do good to those who hate you, and pray for those who spitefully use you and persecute you, that you may be sons of your Father in heaven; for He makes His sun rise on the evil and on the good, and sends rain on the just and on the unjust."
Matthew 5:43-45

Y ou were created to love and be loved. It is impossible to live joyfully without giving and receiving love. It is true. Love hurts. Love anyway. Follow Jesus' example. Remember the Cross. Remember the price He paid to love you. Love also heals.

"Love suffers long." I Corinthians 13:4

Faith Action Step

Reflect on a time when your words or actions hurt someone you loved. The next time someone you love hurts you, remember how you have hurt others, also. Choose to love and forgive.

DAY 27

Spiritual Gifts Do Not Profit without Love

*"And though I bestow all my goods to feed the poor, and though
I give my body to be burned, but have not love, it profits me nothing.
Love suffers long and is kind; love does not envy; love does not pa-
rade itself, is not puffed up; bears all things, believes all things,
hopes all things, endures all things. Love never fails."*
I Corinthians 13:3-4, 7-8, 13

The Corinthian Church to whom Apostle Paul was writing was the most gifted church of all the churches that he established and pastored. They flowed in all the motivational, ministry, and manifestation gifts of the Holy Spirit. They abounded in material wealth as well. Yet, they were also the most sexually immoral, selfish, and strife filled church of all the New Testament churches under the apostolic authority of Apostle Paul.

Furthermore, the Corinthian congregation was the most dishonoring and disrespectful church to their spiritual father. They mocked Paul and dishonored him financially. The Corinthian Christians abounded in spiritual gifts, pride, and gross perversion not even found among sinners. Unfortunately, they demonstrated that spiritual giftedness can function without holiness. Selfishness and impure motives robbed the Corinthian church of their spiritual rewards for the ministry works they performed. Their spiritual gifts were unprofitable for them. The love of Christ was lacking from their motivation to minister their gifts.

What a waste for them. Their absence of Christ-like love and honor for God, their spiritual father, and one another brought shame, disgrace, and grief to Jesus Christ. Sadly, the same selfish spirits present in the Corinthian church are still operating in many churches today.

*"These people draw near to Me with their mouth,
and honor me with their lips but their heart is far from Me.
And in vain they worship Me..." Matthew 15:8*

Faith Action Step
Minister your gifts to the Lord Jesus and the body of Christ with holy hands and a pure heart of Christ's unconditional love.

DAY 28

Stop Worrying

"Therefore, I say to you, do not worry about your life, what you will eat or what you will drink; nor about your body, what you will put on. Is not life more than food and the body more than clothing? "Therefore, do not worry, saying, 'What shall we eat?' or 'What shall we drink?' or 'What shall we wear?' But seek first the kingdom of God and His righteousness, and all these things shall be added to you. Therefore, do not worry about tomorrow, for tomorrow will worry about its own things. Sufficient for the day is its own trouble."
Matthew 6:25,31,33-34

To worry about how your needs will be met is to operate in a spirit of fear and unbelief. You are allowing the evil one to harden your heart and corrupt your confidence in your heavenly Father's love for you. Stop it now! Fear and unbelief are spiritual weeds that choke your faith and open the door to disobedience.

God is the good, good Father. Pull up the evil weeds now. Replant the Word of God in your heart. Daily cultivate and water the implanted Word of God with faith and patience. God promises that you will reap what sow.

"Have faith in God." Mark 11:22

Faith Action Step
Meditate on God's unconditional love for you. Reject the lies of lack the evil one is telling you. Read and meditate on God's love for you in the Gospel of John 3:16 &15:9-17.

DAY 29

Use the Name of Jesus

"If you ask anything in My name, I will do it." John 14:14

There is no other name higher than Jesus. Every name must submit to the authority and power of Jesus Christ. Use the name of Jesus to rid all poverty, lack, pain, sin, sickness, and disease in your life. Use the authority and power Jesus has bequeathed to you and every Christian. Fervently pray to Father God and speak God's promises to the problems in your life.

"Then the seventy returned with joy, saying, "Lord, even the demons are subject to us in Your name." And He said to them, "I saw Satan fall like lightning. Behold, I give you the authority to trample on serpents and scorpions, and over all the power of the enemy, and nothing shall by any means hurt you." Luke 10:17-19

Faith Action Step

Command in the name of Jesus! Command evil to go and blessings to come!

DAY 30

Stay in Your Place

*"If then you were raised with Christ, seek those things
which are above, where Christ is, sitting at the right hand of God."*
Colossians 1:1

Y ou are seated in heavenly places with Christ Jesus far above all prin-
cipalities, powers, and rulers of darkness. You are the head and not
the tail. Keep the evil one under your feet and not in your ear. Do not
listen to his lies. Satan is the father of lies and a murderer from the beginning (John 8:44). Jesus has dethroned, defeated, and destroyed Satan
for you.

*"You are of God, little children, and have overcome them, because
He who is in you is greater than he who is in the world." 1 John 4:4*

Faith Action Step

Live and rule from your heavenly seat of power and authority with
Christ. You are the boss in charge over the evil one.

DAY 31

Raised to Life

"Jesus said to her, "I am the resurrection and the life. He who be-lieves in Me, though he may die, he shall live. Now when He had said these things, He cried with a loud voice, "Lazarus, come forth!" And he who had died came out bound hand and foot with graveclothes, and his face was wrapped with a cloth. Jesus said to them, "Loose him, and let him go." John 11:25, 43-44

The Resurrection power of God is still working. Whatever appears to be dead or dying in your life, God's resurrection power can raise it to life. Can these dry bones live again? Yes, they can. The Word of God has resurrection power. Remain in agreement with Jesus.

"I shall not die, but live, and declare the works of the LORD."
Psalms 118:17

Faith Action Step

Speak the Word of God to the dry bones, situations, and problems in your life. Use the resurrection power of Jesus Christ that He gave to you. Speak spiritual words of life and power to the dead things in your life.

MONTH 2

DAY 32

Bless the Lord

"Bless the Lord, O my soul; And all that is within me, bless His holy name! Bless the Lord, O my soul, and forget not all His benefits."
Psalms 103:1-2

B less means to make happy. It also means to empower to prosper. When you praise God with a grateful heart and give Him thanksgiving for all that He has graciously provided for you, you will make God happy. You also make God happy when you trust and obey His Word. When you bless God, He will bless you more. You can never do more for God than He has done for you. It pleases the Father to bless and multiply you.

"But without faith it is impossible to please Him, for he who comes to God must believe that He is, and that He is a rewarder of those who diligently seek Him." Hebrews 11:6

Faith Action Step

Decide to live a life that is pleasing to God. Do something today to make God happy.

DAY 33

Live God's Way

"If they obey and serve Him, they shall spend
their days in prosperity, and their years in pleasure." Job 36:11

L ife works better when you live like God wills. Trust and obey God. He desires to bless you. Keep living to **p**lease, **o**bey, **s**erve, and **t**rust God (P.O.S.T.). Pleasing God is a lifestyle that leads to overflowing blessings and rewards.

"If you are willing and obedient, you shall eat the good of the land."
Isaiah 1:19

Faith Action Step
With a willing and grateful heart, live a life of obedience to God.

DAY 34

Put a Praise in Your Mouth

"I will bless the Lord at all times.
His Praise shall continually be in my mouth." Psalm 34:1

Jesus longs for your adoration, praise, and thanksgiving. Expressing joyful praise to God from the overflow of a grateful heart is enticing and irresistible to God. Amidst your praise, He will enter the room and sit with you. He will come in the fullness of His glory and fill you with His radiant presence and divine peace.

"Let everything that has breath, praise the Lord". Psalm 150:6

Faith Action Step

Each morning before you rise, spend at least five minutes giving praise and thanksgiving to Jesus. Name your blessings one by one and thank Jesus for everything He has done.

DAY 35

The Weapon of Praise

"Out of the mouths of babes and nursing infants You have ordained perfected praise. Because of Your enemies, that You may silence the enemy and avenger." Matthew 21:16; Psalm 8:2

Praising God is a spiritual weapon that shuts up the evil one. When tormenting thoughts of doubt, anxiety, and depression bombard your mind, put a praise in your mouth. It is humanly impossible for your brain to dwell on a negative thought and sing praises to God at the same time. Your praise can literally draw God's presence near you and drive evil thoughts from you.

"Praise the Lord! Praise God in His sanctuary; Praise Him in His mighty firmament! Praise Him for His mighty acts; Praise Him according to His excellent greatness!" Psalms 150:1-2

Faith Action Step

Make your home a sanctuary of praise to Jesus. Continually play your favorite praise and worship music. Daily sing praise songs to Christ wherever you are.

DAY 36

Guilt Be Gone

"There is therefore now no condemnation to those who are in Christ Jesus, who do not walk according to the flesh, but according to the Spirit." Romans 8:1

Stop condemning yourself with guilt for regrets of the past. God would never condemn you with a guilty conscience. His Son already paid for your guilt with His own blood and body. Honor the blood of Jesus. Refuse to let the enemy put back on you what the blood of Jesus washed away from you.

Forgive and receive God's forgiveness through Jesus Christ. Let the Holy Spirit lead you in all things. Living by the Spirit drives away thoughts and feelings of self-condemnation.

"For if our heart condemns us, God is greater than our heart, and knows all things. Beloved, if our heart does not condemn us, we have confidence toward God. And whatever we ask we receive from Him, because we keep His commandments and do those things that are pleasing in His sight." 1 John 3:20-22

Faith Action Step

Rid yourself of guilt and condemnation forever. Vow to yourself that guilt and condemnation are unwelcome and unacceptable intruders in your life. Evict them today! Command guilt and condemnation to flee from you in Jesus name. Read and memorize Romans 8:1.

Keep speaking and meditating on Romans 8:1 until all traces of guilt and condemnation are gone.

DAY 37

Get Rid of Your Idols

"For you shall worship no other god, for the Lord, whose name is Jealous, is a jealous God," Exodus 34:14

God is a Jealous God. Idols are anything and anyone we prioritize over our time and relationship with God and obedience to Him. Careers, family, lovers, money, ambitions, and activities can become idols. All addictions are idols. Addictions are idols that we substitute for God's presence and comfort. We meditate and run to them for relief and pleasure instead of seeking comfort from God.

God is a Jealous lover. He will not tolerate our divided loyalty and love. He commands us to make Him first place. He commands us to love and trust Him with all our hearts. He will not play second fiddle to anyone or anything. God wants all of you.

"Jesus answered ... 'Hear, O Israel, the Lord our God, the Lord is one. And you shall love the Lord your God with all your heart, with all your soul, with all your mind, and with all your strength.' This is the first commandment." Mark 12:29-30

<u>Faith Action Step</u>

Get rid of your idols. Decide to seek and obey God diligently. Make Him the first and highest priority in your life.

DAY 38

Say Yes to Faith and No to Fear

*"Have I not commanded you? Be strong and of good courage;
do not be afraid, nor be dismayed, for the Lord your God
is with you wherever you go." Joshua 1:9*

Fear is an idol. Remember, idols are anything and anyone we prioritize above obedience to God and our relationship with Him. Fear is a tormenting master. When we obey fear, we are disobeying God. Bible scholars have reported that God has commanded us over 365 times in the Bible to not fear or be afraid. That's one *fear not for each day*. Fear can overcome us when we fail to invest sufficient time in meditating on God's Word and trusting in His love for us.

*"For God has not given us a spirit of fear,
but of power and of love and of a sound mind." II Timothy 1:7*

Faith Action Step

Resolve today to resist allowing fear to control you. Say no to fear and yes to faith. Build and strengthen your faith by reading and trusting the Word of God in the areas where fear is intimidating you. Stand on the promises of God.

DAY 39

Money Is Coming to You

"Submit to God and be at peace with him;
in this way prosperity will come to you." Job 22:21 NIV

Do not work for money. Work for God. Seek God, then let money come to you. If you are serving God wholeheartedly and sowing your treasures, time, talent, and trust into the kingdom of God, then money will seek and pursuit you. The reward of obedience to God is supernatural overflowing divine prosperity. God will command His prosperity to overtake you.

"And you shall again obey the Lord, and observe all His command-
ments which I command you today. Then the Lord your God will
prosper you abundantly in all the work of your hand, in the offspring
of your body and in the offspring of your cattle and in the produce of
your ground, for the Lord will again rejoice over you for good, just as
He rejoiced over your fathers;" Deuteronomy 30:8-9 (NASB)

<u>Faith Action Step</u>
Work for God. Work your job but work the job for God. Choose God as your Source and you will never be unemployed or underpaid. There is no unemployment or underpayment in the kingdom of heaven.

DAY 40

No More Excuses

"Jesus answered and said to him, "If anyone loves Me,
he will keep My word; and My Father will love him, and
We will come to him and make Our home with him." John 14:23

If you want the blessings that God has promised to those who love Him, then you must do the works that God requires those who love Him to do. The works of God are loving, obeying, and trusting Jesus. There are no ifs, ands, or buts about it. You need to trust and obey God. He created you to worship and work for Him. God generously rewards those who trust and obey Jesus.

"If you abide in Me and my words abide in you,
you will ask what you desire and it shall be done for you."
John 15:7

<u>Faith Action Step</u>
Trust and obey. The only way to be happy in Jesus is to trust and obey.

DAY 41

Know Your Season

"To everything there is a season." Ecclesiastes 3:1.

Somethings in your life remain for a season. Somethings remain for life. Some relationships are temporal. Others are eternal. Some ministry assignments are for a season. Some are for life. Know your season. Learn how to move from one season to another gracefully.

"Do not remember the former things, Nor consider the things of old. Behold, I will do a new thing, Now it shall spring forth; Shall you not know it?" Isaiah 43:18-19

Faith Action Step

Thank God for His grace and mercy to enjoy your current season. Ask Holy Spirit for the wisdom and courage to change when it is time for a new season.

DAY 42

Love Leads to Light

"And we know that all things work together for good to those who love God, to those who are the called according to His purpose. He who did not spare His own Son, but delivered Him up for us all, how shall He not with Him also freely give us all things?"
Romans 8:28, 32

Light is revelation of truth. When you are confident in Christ's love for you, you will have divine revelation of the depth of God's goodness towards you. Those who confidently know and receive the love of Christ will have the revelation that Christ has already freely given them all things.

"All things that the Father has are Mine. Therefore, I said that He will take of Mine and declare it to you". John 16:15

Faith Action Step

Memorize and meditate on John 16:15. By faith receive the revelation of it. Just as Heavenly Father has given all that He owns to Jesus, His Heir, Jesus has given everything He owns to us. Christians are joint heirs with Jesus. Read Romans 8:16-18.

DAY 43

Faith Works Through Love

"For in Christ Jesus neither circumcision nor uncircumcision avails anything, but faith working through love." Galatians 5:6

If you are lacking faith in God's love for you, you are lacking in receiving God's promises for you. It is through faith and patience we inherit the promises of God. Knowing and receiving Christ's sacrificial love for us increases our trust in Him and His promises.

"That you do not become sluggish, but imitate those who through faith and patience inherit the promises". Hebrews 6:12

Faith Action Step

Read, meditate, believe, and receive the Scriptures on the love of God for you (John 3:16, John 15:9,13, John 16:27, and John 17:23, 26).

DAY 44

To Love God Is to Obey God

"He who has my commandments and keeps them, it is he who loves Me. And he who loves Me will be loved by My Father, and I will love him and manifest Myself to him." John 14:21

Jesus equates love for Him with obedience to Him. There are so few Christians who truly love Jesus enough to live to please Him as He loved and lived to please His Heavenly Father. Jesus richly rewards obedient Christians whose hearts are loyal to Him. He gives obedient Christians special revelation of Himself, His treasures, and hidden mysteries. God the Father has a special place of affection and honor for those who love His Son with all their heart, soul, mind, and strength.

"For the Father Himself loves you, because you have loved Me and have believed that I came forth from God." John 16:27

Faith Action Step

Commit to loving Jesus with all your heart, soul, mind, and strength. Ask Holy Spirit to teach you how to love Jesus more and more each day.

DAY 45

Let God Bless You

"For I know the plans I have for you," declares the Lord, "plans to prosper you and not to harm you, plans to give you hope and a future. Then you will call on me and come and pray to me, and I will listen to you. You will seek me and find me when you seek me with all your heart. I will be found by you," declares the Lord, "and will bring you back from captivity..." Jeremiah 29:11-14 NIV

God desires and plans to prosper you beyond what you can imagine. However, He needs your cooperation. God needs you to exercise faith and obedience to His Word to prosper you and give you good success in every area of your life. God has made up His mind to bless you. Will you make up your mind to receive His blessings? We receive God's blessings by faith, patience, and obedience to His Word.

"Surely blessing I will bless you and multiplying I will multiply you."
Hebrews 6:14

Faith Action Step

Choose to receive all the blessings that God has reserved for you. Diligently study and apply God's Word to increase your level of faith, patience, and obedience.

DAY 46

Trust God to Provide

"Trust in the Lord with all your heart, And lean not on your own understanding;" Proverbs 3:5

G od has already provided everything that you need to live the life He created you to live. Since God gave you the gifts, talent, and ability to do what He called you to do, He has also provided you with the strength, faith, favor, and finances to do it. Jesus paid it all. Take your mind off yourself. Keep your mind stayed on Jesus. You must step out in faith. By faith in His grace and promises, let God work to complete the work He began in you before you were born. God sees your end from the beginning.

"He who calls you is faithful, who also will do it."
I Thessalonians 5:24

Faith Action Step

Believe that you are more than able to do what God has created you to do. Now by faith in God's Word and grace, go do it.

DAY 47

Live to Obey God

"I call heaven and earth as witnesses today against you, that I have set before you life and death, blessing and cursing; therefore choose life that both you and your descendants may live; that you may love the Lord your God, that you may obey His voice and that you may cling to Him, for He is your life..." Deuteronomy 30:19-20

Live to do God's will. God has a perfect will and a permissive will. It is God's perfect will for all people to worship, serve, and obey His Son, Jesus. However, God's permissive will permits you to receive or reject Jesus. It is God's perfect will for everyone to live happy, healthy, wise, and wealthy. God has set before you life and death. Yet, He has given you the freewill to choose either one. You are free to exercise your own will.

"Not my will but Thy will be done. Thy will be done on earth as it is in heaven. My food is to do the will of Him who sent Me, and to finish His work." Matthew 26:39; Matthew 6:10; John 4:34

Faith Action Step

From this day forward, resolve to live to obey God's will.

DAY 48

Come Closer

"Draw near to God and He will draw near to you." James 4:8

If you feel as though God is far from you, guess what? He is not the one who moved. You are. When you take your eyes off God, your mind and feet will follow. Turn your eyes toward Jesus. Fix your gaze on God, your ever-present help and exceedingly great reward.

"Behold, I stand at the door and knock. If anyone hears My voice and opens the door, I will come in to him and dine with him, and he with Me." Revelation 3:20

Faith Action Step

Open your heart and invite Jesus to come in and fellowship with you.

DAY 49

Guard Your Heart

"Guard your heart above all else, for it determines the course of your life." Proverbs 4:23 NLT

The condition of your heart impacts the outcome of your life. It also impacts those who love you. You live and feed others from the overflow of your heart.

"Your heart is a garden; your thoughts are the seeds.
You can grow fruit, or you can grow weeds.
How will your heart meet other people's needs?"

"A good person produces good things from the treasury of a good heart, and an evil person produces evil things from the treasury of an evil heart." Matthew 12:35 NLT

Faith Action Step

Check your heart. Is it clean and full of unconditional love or is it clogged with impure motives, negative thoughts, and a bad attitude? Ask Holy Spirit, the Divine search engine, to search you and reveal to you the contents of your heart.

DAY 50

Why Is God So Slow?

"O Lord, how long shall I cry, And You will not hear?
Even cry out to You, "Violence!" And You will not save."
Habakkuk 1:2

We can be deceived into believing God moves too slowly for us. However, the truth of the matter is that we move too slowly for God! We are often too slow to believe, too slow to obey, and too slow to understand God's ways.

Consequently, we delay God from releasing our blessings promptly. We go from one level of blessing to another level of blessing based on the growth and maturity of our faith and strength to handle the next level of glory and opposition. The next time you are tempted to think or ask, "Why is God so slow?" Remember to reframe that thought and inquire of yourself, "Why am I so slow to believe, obey, and understand God?"

"The Lord isn't slow to do what he promised, as some people think. Rather, he is patient for your sake. He doesn't want to destroy anyone but wants all people to have an opportunity to turn to him and change the way they think and act." 2 Peter 3:9 GW

Faith Action Step

What do you think, or feel is taking a long time to come to fruition? Honestly evaluate your thoughts and feelings. Are you the person delaying God's answer to your prayer?

DAY 51

Double for Your Trouble

"And the Lord restored Job's losses when he prayed for his friends. Indeed the Lord gave Job twice as much as he had before." Job 42:12

Job received double for his trouble. Satan had suddenly killed Job's children, servants, and livestock. Subsequently, the adversary attacked Job's body with hideous painful boils. Job's wife reacted with bitterness and betrayal. She badgered Job and tried to harass him into cursing God and choosing death. Of course, he resisted her. When it was all said and done, God rewarded Job for maintaining his integrity, unwavering reverence, and trust in God.

When trouble and persecution come, become glad rather than sad. God uses the enemy's theft and persecution for spiritual and material restitution. In Scripture, when a thief steals something from someone, the minimal cost of restitution is double. Zacchaeus, a chief tax collector, promised to give fifty percent of his possessions to the poor and payback four times the amount he collected in taxes if he had cheated anyone (Luke 19:8). Zacchaeus doubled the double.

"Blessed are you when they revile and persecute you and say all kinds of evil against you falsely for My sake. Rejoice and be exceedingly glad, for great is your reward in heaven, for so they persecuted the prophets who were before you." Matthew 5:11-12

Faith Action Step

Change your perspective. In lieu of focusing on the damages and losses you incurred, rejoice and focus on the restitution.

DAY 52

Fear Not

"Why are you fearful, O you of little faith?" Matthew 8:26

Fear contaminates faith. Fear clouds your judgment. Fear inhibits your ability to think and communicate rationally. Fear makes your brain mentally dull. Resist fear. Choose faith. Faith makes you confident, commanding, and courageous.

"Do not be afraid, only believe." Mark 5:36

Faith Action Step

Always seek to choose faith over fear.

DAY 53

Know Your Spiritual Rights.

"Behold, I give you the authority to trample on serpents and scorpions, and over all the power of the enemy, and nothing shall by any means hurt you." Luke 10:19

You need to know your rights before you can exercise your rights. If you have been born of the Holy Spirit through Jesus Christ, then poverty, pain, sin, sickness, disease, and lack possess no legal authority over you. Learn of your Blood Covenant rights in Jesus. Live by faith in your spiritual inheritance.

"All things have been delivered to Me by My Father, and no one knows the Son except the Father. The Spirit Himself bears witness with our spirit that we are children of God, and if children, then heirs—heirs of God and joint heirs with Christ, ..."
Matthew 11:27 & Romans 8:16-17

Faith Action Step

The New Testament of the Holy Bible is the Last Will and Testament of Jesus Christ. Commit to studying it to discover your spiritual inheritance in Christ.

Day 54

Don't Suffer in Silence

*"Come to Me, all you who labor and are heavy laden,
and I will give you rest." Matthew 11:28*

Sometimes life can overwhelm us so much that we find it challenging to think clearly. Good people sometimes make bad decisions. We sometimes make devastating decisions that hurt us and the ones we love. When good hearted people forget how good God is, they will eventually find themselves in trouble. But God is always present and ready to help us to stop the pain, fear, guilt and shame associated with self-destructive behavior. Jesus rescues those who humbly come to Him for help.

*"The Lord is my shepherd; I shall not want. He restores my soul;
He leads me in the paths of righteousness For His name's sake."
Psalms 23:1, 3*

Faith Action Step

Humble yourself. Come to Jesus and ask Him to help, heal, and restore you.

DAY 55

Know the Difference Between Chronological Age and Spiritual Age

"And I, brethren, could not speak to you as to spiritual people but as to carnal, as to babes in Christ. I fed you with milk and not with solid food; for until now you were not able to receive it, and even now you are still not able; for you are still carnal." I Corinthians 3:1-3

Apostle Paul rebuked the Corinthian Christians for their carnality and immaturity. Carnal Christians are babies in the spirit. They only long for the milk of the Word that someone else feeds to them. Carnal Christians live by the desires of their flesh. Their spiritual bellies can only digest milk because they have no teeth or stomach for the solid meat of the Word of God. They only desire teaching that tickles their ears and flatters their soul.

If you are a faith filled adult Christian who is willing to obey and feed on the meat of God's Word day and night, then in the Spirit realm, you can become spiritually mature in merely three and a half years. That's how long it took for Jesus' original 12 Apostles (minus Judas Iscariot) to grow to maturity and inherit Jesus ministry to the world. It's time to grow up and become spiritually mature Christians. Get off the baby bottle. Take off the diapers. Put on and keep on your grown-up spiritual armor wear.

"For though by this time you ought to be teachers, you need someone to teach you again the first principles of the oracles of God; and you have come to need milk and not solid food. For everyone who partakes only of milk is unskilled in the word of righteousness, for he is a babe. But solid food belongs to those who are of full age, that is, those who by reason of use have their senses exercised to discern both good and evil." Hebrews 5:12-14

Faith Action Step

Refuse to remain a spiritual babe. Feed yourself the meat of God's Word every day!

DAY 56

Faith Comes by Hearing

"So then faith comes by hearing, and hearing by the word of God."
Romans 10:17

What you repeatedly hear, you are prone to believe. Far too many of us still believe the negative words people have spoken to us from our childhood. "You're too slow. You're too smart. Nobody likes a know it all. You're too dark. You're too light. You're too fat. You're too skinny. You're too short. You're too tall. You're too nerdy. You're too mean. You're too hyper. You're too lazy. You're too religious. "

Whether it's negative faith or godly faith, they both come by hearing powerful words repetitively spoken to you. Eventually, you will believe and internalize what you hear. Continually hearing God's Word until you believe it, will uproot the negative childhood beliefs that you have internalized.

"And since we have the same spirit of faith, according to what is written, "I believed and therefore I spoke," we also believe and therefore speak." II Corinthians 4:13

Faith Action Step

Read, study, meditate, and speak the Word to yourself until you become one with the Word of God. Practice thinking and saying the Word of God until the Word automatically becomes your thoughts and your words.

DAY 57

Free at Last

"Then Jesus said to those Jews who believed Him, "If you abide in My word, you are My disciples indeed. And you shall know the truth, and the truth shall make you free." Therefore, if the Son makes you free, you shall be free indeed." John 8:31-32

If the Spirit of Christ dwells in you, then you are free. You are free from the power and penalty of sin. You are free from the power of money, ungodly lusts, and all the power of the enemy. You are free from fear, anxiety, and depression. You are free at last.

"Therefore, if the Son makes you free, you shall be free indeed."
John 8:36

Faith Action Step

Thank God Almighty that you are free! Now believe that you are free from the power of everything that seeks to control you.

DAY 58

Stay Free

"Stand fast therefore in the liberty by which Christ has made us free, and do not be entangled again with a yoke of slavery (bondage)."
Galatians 5:1

Make your position and practice the same. Your position in Christ Jesus is a free man or free woman. Christ has made you free positionally. Now live free practically. With freedom comes much responsibility. Some people prefer bondage rather than freedom.

The Hebrews, in the book of Exodus, had been enslaved to Egypt for 400 years before Pharaoh finally released them. However, as they journeyed to the Promise Land under God's appointed leader and deliverer, Moses, many of the freed Hebrew slaves began to murmur, complain, and treacherously spoke of wanting to return to Egypt. When faced with the responsibility of having to trust God instead of Pharaoh for their provisions, they preferred their former bondage instead of their new freedom.

You have been translated out of the kingdom of darkness and slavery into God's kingdom of light and abundance. Reject the lies of the evil one to lure you back into bondage. Through Christ's victory, the enemy lost his power over you.

"Now the Lord is the Spirit, and where the Spirit of the Lord is, there is freedom." 2 Corinthians 3:17 NIV

<u>Faith Action Step</u>
Live free. Stay free. Choose to live in the Light. Appreciate the favor of God. Refuse to frustrate His grace.

DAY 59

Be Grateful

"Honor the Lord with your possessions and with the first fruits of all your increase. So your barns will be filled with plenty and your vats will overflow with new wine." Proverbs 3:9-10

The attitude of gratitude is much more than saying a polite thank you to someone rendering service to you. The greatest expression of gratitude that you can give to someone who has blessed or served you is a monetary or material gift to demonstrate your appreciation and thanksgiving. The waiter or waitress who courteously and faithfully served you at your favorite restaurant will expect a gracious tip of money with your words of thanksgiving.

Faith, family, friends, health, education, jobs, spiritual, and political freedom are gifts and blessings from God. Honor God with at least a tenth of all your income and increase for how He abundantly blesses you. Some people tip waiters and waitresses a higher percentage of their bill than they tithe to God.

Taking God's gifts for granted and losing those gifts because of ingratitude is a very painful life lesson. Sometimes what you have lost because of thanklessness, God will restore. Sometimes you will have to accept the loss and move forward. Learn from it and commit to change. You will need to forgive yourself, ask and receive God's forgiveness for your ingratitude, and ask the person who you took for granted to forgive you. Pray the Serenity prayer frequently for the strength to accept what happened. Now move forward. Commit to think and live gratefully.

"You shall truly tithe all the increase of your grain that the field produces year by year. And all the tithe of the land, whether of the seed of the land or of the fruit of the tree, is the Lord's. It is holy to the Lord." Deuteronomy 14:22; Leviticus 27:30

Faith Action Step

Develop an attitude of gratitude. Thank God for each new day and the family, friends, health, and material blessings He has given to you.

DAY 60

It Is Impossible for God to Forget You

"Can a woman forget her child at the breast, not show pity on the child from her womb? Even if these were to forget, I would not forget you. I have engraved you on the palms of my hands, your walls are always before me." Isaiah 49:15-16 CJB

God always remembers you. He remembers every good deed and every good seed you have sown. He loves you far too much to forget you. He loves you with an everlasting love and an insatiable desire to bless you. Your prosperity and good success are always on his mind (Jeremiah 29:11-12). He will bless you. He will multiply you. He will bless and multiply you, your children, and your children's children (Genesis 22:17). Believe He has you on His mind.

"For God is not unjust to forget your work and labor of love which you have shown toward His name, in that you have ministered to the saints and do minister." Hebrews 6:10

Faith Action Step

Remember God is your good, good, Heavenly Father. Trust in His love and mercy.

DAY 61

Time Waits for No One

*"So teach us to number our days,
that we may gain a heart of understanding." Psalm 90:12*

Have you noticed lately that the days seem to come and go faster than last year? Well, it is true. The days will be shortened. "And unless those days were shortened, no flesh would be saved; but for the elect's sake those days will be shortened." (Matt. 24:22). Use your time wisely to prioritize and invest your energy in what matters most to you. Once the day is gone, it is gone forever.

*"Therefore, pay careful attention to how you conduct your life — live wisely, not unwisely. Use your time well, for these are evil days."
Ephesians 5:15-16 CJB*

Faith Action Step

Ask God to show you how you can better manage your time to invest in reading and meditating on His Word more. Diligently seek Him in prayer to receive His divine instructions daily. Trust He will help you to prioritize your time to accomplish His plans for each day.

MONTH 3

DAY 62

What's Your Strong Tower?

"The name of the Lord is a strong tower;
The righteous run to it and are safe." Proverbs 18:10

Towers represent safety and storage. When storms are raging in your life, you have a safe place to run and hide. When your supply of strength, faith, and finances run low, you have a storage place to which you can go. Jesus is your strong tower. He is your hiding place. He has a storehouse for all who seek Him.

"The Lord will open for you His good storehouse, the heavens, to give rain to your land in its season and to bless all the work of your hand; and you shall lend to many nations, but you shall not borrow."
Deuteronomy 28:12

Faith Action Step
Practice visualizing running to Jesus for safety from the stress producing storms in your life. Jesus is your safe place.

DAY 63

God Is Greater Than Your Problems

"You are of God, little children, and have overcome them, because He who is in you is greater than he who is in the world." I John 4:4

The power and promises of your God are greater than the problems you perceive. Meditate on His divine promises in place of your perceived problems. You will think and feel better if you consider problems as faith strengthening opportunities to exercise overcoming faith.

"Therefore, humble yourselves under the mighty hand of God, that He may exalt you in due time, casting all your care upon Him for He cares for you." I Peter 5:7

Faith Action Step

Choose to meditate on one of the many Scriptural promises that I have shared in this devotional. Speak and meditate on it when you rise each morning and each night before going to sleep. The Word of God can change your negative perspective.

DAY 64

The Prayer of Petition

"Now this is the confidence that we have in Him, that if we ask anything according to His will, He hears us. And if we know that He hears us, whatever we ask, we know that we have the petitions that we have asked of Him." I John 5:14-15

Have you ever signed a group petition requesting an official to change a law? Have you ever had to appear in Court to petition a judge to grant your request to rule in your favor? A petition is an official written request addressed and presented to a person in authority who has the power to grant or deny the request. According to the spiritual laws of your covenant of wealth in Christ Jesus, you can write a petition to God, the Father, and ask Him to fulfill a specific Scriptural promise for you. By His spiritual law, He will grant your request.

"All the promises of God are yes and Amen." 2 Corinthians 1:20

<u>Faith Action Step</u>

Write, date, sign, pray, and present your Scripture promises to God today. By faith, receive His ruling of yes.

DAY 65

The Weight of the Wait

*"And let us not grow weary while doing good, for in due
season we shall reap if we do not lose heart." Galatians 6:9*

Two decades ago, I heard my good friend, Dr. Haywood Robinson,
III, preach a message entitled the *Weight of the Wait*. To this day, the
Lord uses these same words to minister to me as they did when I first
heard them. Perhaps you can relate to the heaviness of the soul as you
bear up under the *Weight of the Wait*. Your spirit is willing to wait on God
for however long it may take. Yet, your soul is weak and can become
weary of the waiting process. Developing patience may seem to be an
arduous task. However, maturity in patience is a necessity to complete
your journey to the Promise Land.

It is by faith and patience we inherit the promises of God. I encourage
you to rejoice in the Lord for the process. You are closer now than you
ever were before to inheriting His promises. Be of good cheer! You are
almost there.

*"Wait on the Lord; Be of good courage, and
He shall strengthen your heart. Wait, I say, on the Lord!"
Psalm 27:14*

Faith Action Step
Resist unbelief and weariness. They will rob you of God's exceedingly
great and precious promises. Keep your faith focused on the faithfulness
of God.

9/4/19

DAY 66

Stop Worrying

"Therefore, I say to you, do not worry about your life, what you will eat or what you will drink; nor about your body, what you will put on. Is not life more than food and the body more than clothing? "Therefore, do not worry, saying, 'What shall we eat?' or 'What shall we drink?' or 'What shall we wear?'" Matthew 6:25, 31

Throughout the Bible, God commands us not to fear. Unbelief and self-centeredness are the roots of fear and evil. Worrying is the sin of unbelief and fear. The definition of sin is the **S**elf-centered **I**ndependent **N**ature (S.I.N.). Thus, fear and unbelief produce the unrighteous fruit of disobedience.

The anxious heart and mind do not believe and trust God to perform His Word. People are more inclined to obey those whom they trust. Sadly, the human nature would rather believe and trust in itself than to believe and trust God. Christians need to live from their **S**on **of** God Nature (S.O.N.) in lieu of their **S**elf-centered **I**ndependent **N**ature.

"But seek first the kingdom of God and His righteousness, and all these things shall be added to you. Therefore, do not worry about tomorrow, for tomorrow will worry about its own things. Sufficient for the day is its own trouble." "Have faith in God." Matthew 6:33-34 and Mark 11:22

Faith Action Step

1. Make two columns on an 8 ½ x 11 sheet of paper. Label the first column Worries. Label column 2, Promises.

2. In the Worries column, write the top 10 things that you worry about often.

3. In the Promises column, write a Scripture promise to counteract each worry.

4. Fold the paper in half vertically. Tear it into two separate sheets.

5. Rip the Worries list into pieces. Throw them in the trash.

6. Hold onto the Promises of God list. Whenever you are attempted to worry, read aloud the Scripture promise to counteract the worry.

DAY 67

Do You Have Heart Trouble?

"DO NOT let your hearts be troubled (distressed, agitated). You believe in and adhere to and trust in and rely on God; believe in and adhere to and trust in and rely also on Me." John 14:1 AMPC

The cure for a troubled heart is to believe God's Word. Encountering trouble is a part of life. Trouble is an indication that you are alive. As long as you live in the earth, you will experience problems. But God is still on His throne. He is incapable of abandoning or forgetting you.

"In the world you will have tribulation;
but be of good cheer, I have overcome the world." John 16:33

<u>Faith Action Step</u>
Praise and worship God in trouble and turmoil. Ask Heavenly Father, to help you. Thank Him for His goodness and mercy.

DAY 68

Heart Soil

"For out of the abundance of the heart the mouth speaks. A good man out of the good treasure of his heart brings forth good things, and an evil man out of the evil treasure brings forth evil things."
Matthew 12:34-35

Your heart is spiritual soil where words and thoughts are planted. The condition of the soil determines the quality and quantity of the harvests. Good seed needs to be sown in good soil. Is your heart good soil?

The Word of God is good incorruptible seed. It will produce exponentially in a good heart. It will produce sparingly in a hard heart of fear and unbelief. If you are lacking the abundance in your life that you desire, then check the condition of your heart soil. Is your heart fertile soil?

"The sower sows the Word. But these are the ones sown on good ground, those who hear the word, accept it, and bear fruit: some thirtyfold, some sixty, and some a hundred." Mark 4:14,20

Faith Action Step

Intentionally pay attention to your words. Are you speaking the Scriptures more than you are speaking your own words? Are your words more positive than negative? Are you speaking abundance more than lack? Analyze what you hear yourself saying.

DAY 69

The Joy of Sowing

"God loves a cheerful giver." 2 Corinthians 9:7

Jesus said, "It is better to give than to receive". The joy of giving is contagious. It is an awesome privilege to receive God's favor and special calling to become a cheerful giver. Givers are His special representatives to demonstrate His love through the grace of giving. It is a humbly and rewarding call. When we bless people by meeting their physical needs and desires, we love, live, serve, and share like Christ. They reciprocate by blessing and glorifying our Heavenly Father with much thanksgiving and praise for His goodness. Jesus commands us to be His witnesses to the world of the goodness of God. By our generous giving, good works, and sharing the good news of salvation in Jesus Christ, we become His witnesses.

"Let your light so shine before men, that they may see your good works and glorify your Father in heaven." Matthew 5:16

Faith Action Step

Ask Holy Spirit to help you to show the generosity and goodness of God to three people today. Give a gift, a compliment, or do a kind deed for three different people today.

DAY 70

People are not thinking about you as much as you think they are

"Set your mind on things above, not on things on the earth."
Colossians 3:2

Most people are preoccupied with their own lives and problems. The pressures and cares of this world invades most of their waking thoughts. Worrying about life, leaves them little room to mediate on how they may have offended you. So be quick to forgive and forget offenses against you. Avoid living in the past. The past is gone.

"Brethren, I do not count myself to have apprehended; but one thing I do, forgetting those things which are behind and reaching forward to those things which are ahead, I press toward the goal for the prize of the upward call of God in Christ Jesus." Philippians 3:13-14

Faith Action Step

Live in the present. Stop rehearsing past hurts and mistakes. Move forward.

DAY 71

Sometimes You Have to Walk Alone

Jesus said, "Do not think that I came to bring peace on earth. I did not come to bring peace but a sword. For I have come to 'set a man against his father, a daughter against her mother, and a daughter-in-law against her mother-in-law'; and 'a man's enemies will be those of his own household.' He who loves father or mother more than Me is not worthy of Me. And he who loves son or daughter more than Me is not worthy of Me." Matthew 10:34-37

On your journey to spiritual success, you will have to leave people behind. Many who began the pilgrimage with you, will end it prematurely. You must accept that the journey is your own. Not everyone you love wants to go where you are going. Please understand. People are either progressing or regressing. Regression hinders progression.

Who is hindering your progress? Who do you need to leave in the past? Family loyalty comes second to your devotion and obedience to Jesus. The sobering truth is this: You can invite them to come but, you must **let them choose**.

Jesus said, "Who is My mother, or My brothers? Here are My mother and My brothers! For whoever does the will of God is My brother and My sister, and mother." Mark 3:33-35

Faith Action Step

Cast off the dead weights. Keep moving forward. Run your race with God's grace.

DAY 72

Peace and Happiness Are the Fruits of Trust in God

"You will keep him in perfect peace, whose mind is stayed on You, Because he trusts in You. Trust in the Lord forever, For in YAH, the Lord, is everlasting strength." Isaiah 26:3-4

The people who truly and completely trust in God's love and Word will have an abundance of peace and happiness. In the absence of trust in God is fear, worry, and discouragement. A lack of peace comes from a lack of trust in God. Develop the discipline and determination to keep your mind focused steadfastly on the goodness of God. Focusing on God's love will keep your mind in peace rather than in pieces.

"Happy are those who trust in the Lord, who rely on the Lord." Jeremiah 17:7 CEB

Faith Action Step

Commit to trust and rely on God's Word. Reject emotional reasoning. Only believe and trust what the Word of God says.

DAY 73

Jesus Is with You

"Fear not, for I have redeemed you; I have called you by your name; You are Mine. When you pass through the waters, I will be with you; And through the rivers, they shall not overflow you. When you walk through the fire, you shall not be burned, Nor shall the flame scorch you." Isaiah 43:1,2

Decide to take Jesus with you everywhere you go. To do so will bring the glory of God into every place that you dwell, work, worship, or visit. The glory of God is the radiant manifestation of God's goodness, presence, power, majesty, and wealth. When God's glory enters a place, His brightness will dispel all darkness and evil. The weight of His glory will bring and attract wealth and favor.

"Arise, shine; For your light has come! And the glory of the Lord is risen upon you." Isaiah 60:1

Faith Action Step
Consistently practice seeking the presence of God in your private and public worship. Thus, the presence of God will attract others to seek and favor you.

DAY 74

Jesus' Name is Your Name

"For this reason, I bow my knees to the Father of our Lord Jesus Christ, from whom the whole family in heaven and earth is named,"
Ephesians 3:14-15

As a husband gives his wife his name, Jesus gives His bride, the Church, His name. The Bride of Christ is called by His name, Christian. All that the husband legally owns in his name belongs to the wife because she shares his name. A man's new wife becomes a joint owner with all rights and authority to what he owns and vice versa. As soon as I became Mrs. Paul Chipman, all my husband's earthly goods became mine. Shortly before I married him, I had purchased a brand-new car. When I married my husband, I added his name to the title deed of my car. He legally inherited my new car. What was once mine, became ours. Likewise, the church of Jesus is His spiritual bride. We are joint heirs with Christ to all that He owns. Jesus said,

"All things that the Father has are Mine. Therefore, I said that He will take of Mine and declare it to you." John 16:15

Faith Action Step

Purpose in your heart to receive and enjoy all the fullness of your legal spiritual inheritance as the Church, the Bride of Christ.

DAY 75

Let Jesus Dress You

"So why do you worry about clothing? Now if God so clothes the grass of the field, which today is, and tomorrow is thrown into the oven, will He not much more clothe you, O you of little faith?" Matthew 6:28,30

God is the good, good Heavenly Father. So why worry about food and clothing? Only irresponsible parents would care less about their children's material needs. Do you honestly think your Heavenly Father is a dead-beat Dad?

Your Heavenly Father loves you as much as He loves His only begotten Son, Jesus. Heavenly Father has given everything to His Son to richly enjoy. Jesus has given everything to His Church that the Father has given to Him. He confidently received all His inheritance that His Father bestowed upon Him. Boldly, receive your joint-heir status with Jesus.

"But put on the Lord Jesus Christ, for in Him dwells all the fullness of the Godhead bodily." Romans 13:14 and Colossians 2:9

Faith Action Step

Follow the example of Jesus. Confidently receive by faith the full inheritance that Jesus has given to you.

DAY 76

It's All in Your Mind

"Is anything too hard for God?" Genesis 18:14

Your mindset determines your perspective. Perspective affects every-thing. One person's problem is another person's opportunity. Is the glass half full or half empty? It all depends on your perspective. Are problems really problems or opportunities to depend on God's Word for creative solutions? Your perspective will determine your outcome.

"I can do all things through Christ who strengthens me."
Philippians 4:13

Faith Action Step

Change your perspective. Ask Holy Spirit to show you the mind of Christ to overcome the challenges in your life.

DAY 77

Why is God Taking So Long?

"Men always ought to pray and not lose heart. There was in a certain city a judge who did not fear God nor regard man. Now there was a widow in that city, and she came to him saying, 'Get justice for me from my adversary'. And he would not for a while, but afterwards he said within himself, "Though I do not fear God nor regard man, yet because this widow troubles me I will avenge her, lest by her continual coming she weary me." Luke 18:1-5

When it seems like our prayers or desires are delayed, we often assume the problem is with God. However, the Bible teaches that the prayers that we pray, God works through people to answer them. People are often the delay for God's answer to your prayer. For example, examine your own response to God when Holy Spirit prompts you to call, pray for, sow a large sum of money into someone or give them your car, favorite clothes, shoes or jewelry. How long do you take to obey? How many times does Holy Spirit have to keep speaking and nudging you to release what He told you to give or do what He told you to do? People are prone to procrastinate. Procrastination delays our answered prayers.

"Let him who is taught the Word share in all good things with him who teaches. Do not be deceived, God is not mocked; for whatever a man sows, that he will also reap. Therefore, as we have opportunity, let us do good to all, especially to those who are of the household of faith." Galatians 6:6, 7, 9

Faith Action Step

The next time you are tempted to think, feel, or ask, "What's taking God so long?", ask Holy Spirit, "How am I or someone else delaying my blessing?"

DAY 78

The Spiritual Law of Restitution

"You will receive a double measure of wealth instead of your shame. You will sing about your wealth instead of being disgraced. That is why you will have a double measure of wealth in your land. You will have everlasting joy." Isaiah 61:7 GW

In the Old Testament, the biblical law of restitution required a thief to pay back to the wronged person, a minimum penalty of double what they stole to a maximum penalty of seven times the value of what was stolen. The evil one is a thief. Exercise your legal spiritual rights. Make your petition before Jesus, the Lawgiver and Righteous Judge, and demand a verdict of the maximum penalty for the trouble the adversary has caused you. God will make the enemy pay you damages for all the trouble he caused you.

"Keep asking and it shall be given to you; keep searching and you shall find; keep knocking and the delet (door) shall be opened to you." Matthew 7:7 OJB

Faith Action Step

Keep petitioning and demanding until Jesus gives you the justice you desire.

DAY 79

You Are Good Enough

*"Then God saw everything that He made,
and indeed it was very good." Genesis 1:31*

God is good. God saw that everything He made was very good. Since God made you, you are very good. You are made like God, by God, and for God. Therefore, God predetermined your worth and value long before you were born. You are more than good enough for God to bless you and use you to serve Him. Your gifts and calling are predetermined. God thought, planned, and wrote in His books what works He had already chosen for you to do. God's plans are irrevocable.

*"For the gifts and the calling of God are irrevocable.
For we are His workmanship, created in Christ Jesus for good works,
which God prepared beforehand that we should walk in them."
Romans 11:29 & Ephesians 2:10*

Faith Action Step

Believe the good that God says about you is true. Believe the report of the Lord.

DAY 80

It's Time to Put Away Childish Thinking and Childish Behavior

"When I was a child, I spoke as a child, I understood as a child, I thought as a child; but when I became a man, I put away childish things." I Corinthians 13:11

Little toddlers and preschoolers are the most self-centered and hedonistic humans in the world. They inherently believe the world revolves around them. Toddlers believe their parents and family live to serve them. Toddlers live for pleasure and play. They want what they want when they want it 'or else'. The 'or else' typically manifests in outbursts of crying, fits of anger, and or tantrums when they don't get what they want.

It's sad to say but, God has some big adult children who act like toddlers when their heavenly Father does not give them what they want, how they want it, or when they want it. Tantrums are a manifestation of immaturity. Natural babies and spiritual babies throw tantrums. It's time to grow up in the Lord.

"But grow in the grace and knowledge of our Lord and Savior Jesus Christ. To Him be the glory both now and forever. Amen."
2 Peter 3:14

Faith Action Step

Decide now to grow up spiritually. Eliminate soulish junk food. Feed your spirit the Word of God to grow and build up your faith in God.

DAY 81

Jesus Is Your Leader-Follow Your Leader

Then He said to them, "Follow Me and
I will make you fishers of men." Matthew 4:19

Leaders are leaders if they have followers. Jesus commanded His disciples to follow Him. True leaders will walk and talk with the authority that God has given them and deliver the results of their calling. Given that the twelve apostles were Jewish, they understood that to follow Jesus as their Rabbi, meant Jesus gave them an invitational command to leave everything behind. They understood Jesus was commanding them to come join His party to be faithful to follow Him wherever He went. The apostles grasped the profundity of the costs of discipleship. That cost would require them to sacrifice their occupations, family, and dreams to become a disciple (follower, student) of Christ.

Jesus was true to His word. He summoned a group of twelve angry, uneducated, self-centered, self-ambitious, and self-aggrandizing men whom He converted into world transforming apostles. They possessed supernatural wisdom, power, and convicting leadership. Except for one, the traitor, they all became just like the Master Teacher. They faithfully followed and served Jesus until their deaths. What price are you willing to pay to become a true follower and student of Jesus Christ?

Jesus said, "A disciple is not above his teacher, nor a servant above his master. It is enough for a disciple that he be like his teacher, and a servant like his master... And he who does not take his cross and follow after me is not worthy of Me. But Jesus said to him, "Follow Me and let the dead bury their own dead." Matthew 10:24-25, 38; Matthew 8:22

Faith Action Step
Determine to love and live like Jesus. Follow the Leader.

DAY 82

Jesus Wants You Joyful

"Rejoice in the Lord always! For the joy of the Lord is your strength." Philippians 4:4 & Nehemiah 8:10

Jesus wants you joyful! God answers our prayers to increase our joy (John 16:24). Sadness, anxiety, and depression zaps you of your strength. However, joy gives you strength. Happiness is a fleeing emotional state that is contingent upon fluctuating circumstances and external events. Yet, joy is an unalterable spiritual character of internal gratitude and contentment. Joy like love is unconditional. Joy is the fruit of the Holy Spirit. Jesus want us to increase in His love, joy, and peace.

"But let the righteous be glad; Let them rejoice before God; Yes, let them rejoice exceedingly. Sing to God, sing praises to His name; Extol Him who rides on the clouds, By His name Yah, And rejoice before Him." Psalms 68:3-4

Faith Action Step

Rejoice in the Lord always!

DAY 83

Stay in Alignment with the Word of God

"If you abide in Me, and My words abide in you, ask whatever you wish, and it will be done for you." John 15:7 NASB

Exercising faith means to keep yourself in alignment and agreement with God's Word. When the front end is out of alignment on my car, it adversely affects other parts of the car, too. My steering wheel pulls to the left and sometimes vibrates. If I delay getting the car aligned, then my tires will wear out sooner than I expect. Similarly, when we allow our lives to become out of alignment with God's Word, it adversely affects our ability to steer straight towards God's destiny. The enemy attempts to pull on our spiritual steering wheel to hinder our navigation and ability to keep moving forward. Straight and narrow is the road that leads to life.

Broad is the road that leads to destruction. The evil one uses temptations, troubles, and distractions to lure us away from following God's Word. When we traverse the populated Broad road, we are living out of alignment with God. Eventually, we will pull our network of relationships out of alignment too. In your physical body, when one member is dysfunctional, the whole body becomes dysfunctional. Other organs, systems and members need to work harder to compensate for the dysfunctional member's slack. The body of Christ is one body and one family. When one member of the body or family is spiritually misaligned, the whole body and family becomes misaligned.

"A little leaven leavens the whole lump" (Galatians 5:9). Living a Word driven life opposed to a world driven life is an unpopular way to live. Few are willing to walk its narrow path. The road of the Word is the road less traveled.

"Examine yourselves to see if your faith is genuine. Test yourselves... if not, you have failed the test of genuine faith." 2 Corinthians 13:5 NLT

Faith Action Step

Work steadfastly to keep your spirit, soul, and body trusting and obeying God's Word and doing God's will. Jesus said to them, "My food is to do the will of Him who sent Me, and to finish His work." John 4:34

DAY 84

Weeping Sometimes Precedes Joy

"Weeping may endure for a night, but joy comes in the morning"
Psalm 30:5

Joy arises when you focus on the bountiful blessings to come instead of the suffering at hand. Sometimes when you feel like weeping, God will require a sacrifice of praise. Praise Him anyhow! Weeping drains you. Joy strengthens you.

In the middle of your praise, God will turn your sorrow into joy. His gift of joy will preserve you. When you feel weak, God will make you strong. He will turn your mourning into a song. God will not delay. Your harvest of joy is on the way.

"Those who sow in tears Shall reap in joy. He who continually goes forth weeping, Bearing seed for sowing, Shall doubtless come again with rejoicing, Bringing his sheaves with him." Psalms 126:5-6

Faith Action Step

Keep sowing and rejoicing!

DAY 85

Be Sure to Serve the Lord with Joy and Gladness

"Because you did not serve the Lord your God with joy and gladness of heart, for the abundance of everything, therefore you shall serve your enemies whom the Lord will send against you, in hunger, in thirst, in nakedness and in need of everything;" Deuteronomy 28:47

God hates ingratitude. If you really want to get on God's nerves, then complain and grumble about your life. Complaining, murmuring, and grumbling about how bad things are or what is lacking in your life is a definite invitation for God to withdraw His hand of blessing from you.

What began as a forty-day journey to spy out the Promise Land of overflowing blessings for the children of Israel, became a forty-year nightmare of death and destruction in the Wilderness of Paran. The entire generation from age twenty and above died in the wilderness except for Caleb and Joshua. These two men served Moses faithfully and believed the report of the Lord. What happened?

God became infuriated with the doubt, unbelief, and complaining from the children of Israel. They did not believe Caleb and Joshua's report from the Lord that they could possess the Promise Land. Ultimately, God sentenced the unbelieving congregation one year for each forty days the twelve spies searched the Promise Land (Numbers 14:26,34). The Lord was angry at them for their constant disbelief and rejection of Him and His good plans for them. In His wrath, God condemned an entire generation in the wilderness, except for the two men who believed Him, Caleb and Joshua. God saved a remnant of two men. He saved one man per one million people that He condemned (Numbers 14:38).

"Do all things without complaining and disputing, that you may become blameless and harmless, children of God without fault in the midst of a crooked and perverse generation, among whom you shine as lights in the world." Philippian 2:14-15

Faith Action Step

Stop murmuring and complaining. Be grateful to God for everything you have.

DAY 86

Walk by Faith in What You Heard

*"Your ears shall hear a word behind you saying,
"This is the way, walk in it," whenever you turn to the
right hand or whenever you turn to the left." Isaiah 30:21*

The Bible is the logos, the written Word of God. When Holy Spirit speaks the logos to you for a specific reply or response to what's going on in your life, that logos becomes a rhema for you. The rhema word of Holy Spirit is your confirmation from God. Many years ago, I was having a financial struggle and lacked the money to buy some things I wanted. At the time, Holy Spirit led me to read Isaiah 55 from the beginning of the chapter instead of beginning at verse 5 as I usually would. Isaiah 55:1 reads,

"Ho! Everyone who thirsts, come to the waters; and you who have no money, come, buy and eat. Yes, come buy wine and milk without money and without price."

That logos became a rhema word for me personally. On that precise day, I received the revelation and true meaning of Jesus paid it all! I have an everlasting covenant with my Heavenly Father through Jesus Christ, His Son. Finally, I understood the depth of the mystery of Matthew 6:33. If I keep my primary focus on pursing God's kingdom agenda for the world and His righteousness (God's ways of thinking, being, and doing right), then God will certainly give me all that I need and desire to accomplish His will for my life.

The revelation of Isaiah 55:1 & 3 and Matthew 6:33 freed me from financial worry and pressure. The realization that God will finance His own kingdom work was astonishingly liberating. God's responsibility is to pay for it. My responsibility is to pray and believe for it. It is really a true statement that "Where God guides, God provides." If God said it and you truly believe it, it will surely come to pass.

*"My sheep hear My voice, and I know them and they follow Me."
John 10:27*

Faith Action Step
Seek the kingdom of God and His righteousness first. Trust that everything else will be added to you.

DAY 87

Talk Less, Work More

"In all labor there is profit, but idle chatter leads only to poverty."
Proverbs 14:23

Whatever you want, you will achieve by work. Do the faith work, mental work, relational work, and physical work. When you do the required work, you will receive the desired reward.

"The hand of the diligent makes rich. Do you see a man who excels in his work? He will stand before kings. He will not stand before unknown men." Proverbs 10:4 and Proverbs 22:29

Faith Action Step
Commit to believe and do the due diligence to accomplish your goals.

DAY 88

Grow Your Faith

"For in it the righteousness of God is revealed from faith to faith; as it is written, "The just shall live by faith." Romans 1:17

As your faith in Jesus matures, your faith will grow from the foundational level of saving faith, to sense faith, to strong faith to the highest level, supernatural faith. All levels of faith in God and His Word come by exercising saving faith in Jesus Christ. To save means to rescue, to deliver from death and danger. Jesus Christ is the Savior of the world. He alone is without sin and has the redeeming and resurrection power to save all humans from the penalty of sin.

Saving faith is the gift of God. God gives it (deposits it into your spirit) when you repent from sin and receive forgiveness from Jesus. It is the free gift of God. However, to grow and work your faith is your responsibility. Jesus gave it, but you must grow it.

Sense faith is believing and acting on God's Word if it makes sense or feels right. Sense faith is a diluted faith. It relies on logic and the natural senses to corroborate the Word of God. Reliance on the soul is the foundation of sense faith.

Contrarily, strong faith believes and acts on the Word of God without necessitating the natural senses to validate its veracity. It is pure undiluted faith. Strong faith stands on the promises of God inwardly without requiring any outward sign to confirm the Word of God. Human intellect and reasoning are non-variables to those who live by strong faith.

Supernatural faith is the highest level of faith. It is undeterred and unaffected by natural laws, human wisdom, or worldly power. To live by supernatural faith is to live a life characterized by human impossibilities. Supernatural faith enables Christians to love, live, serve and share just like Jesus (John 14:12-14).

"For with God nothing will be impossible." Luke 1:47

Faith Action Step

Keep growing your faith.

DAY 89

Righteousness Is the Currency in the Kingdom of God

"Therefore, do not worry, saying 'What shall we eat?' or 'What shall we drink?' or 'What shall we wear?' But seek first the kingdom of God and His righteousness, and all these things shall be added to you." Matthew 6:33

Every kingdom or country has its own currency. The currency of the United States of America is the dollar. The Russian currency is the ruble. The Dubai currency is the dirham. The value of the currency is predicated upon where you are shopping. When I traveled to Russia, 1 dollar was worth approximately 56 rubles. The Russian ruble was worth slightly more than .02 cents of 1 U.S. dollar. One dollar in Dubai was worth 3.67 dirhams. In Dubai, I purchased items with my American dollars without needing to exchange. However, in Russia I had to exchange my American money into Russian money to purchase products.

Likewise, to transact business in the kingdom of God, you must have the correct currency. Material money is worthless in a spiritual kingdom. You need spiritual currency. The righteousness of God that comes through faith in Jesus Christ is the right currency. The kingdom of God is an abundant kingdom overflowing with everything that you need or desire. Increase practicing the righteousness of God and you will increase your buying power in the kingdom of God. Jesus fed over 5,000 people on more than one occasion. He had a huge supply of righteousness with exponential purchasing power. In the kingdom of God, you have the same purchasing power as Jesus.

"The generation of the upright will be blessed. Wealth and riches will be in his house, and his righteousness endures forever." Psalms112:2-3

Faith Action Step

Embrace your righteousness. Remember, the righteousness of God is God's ways of thinking, being, and doing right.

DAY 90

Help to Pray

"Likewise, the Spirit also helps in our weaknesses. For we do not know what we should pray for as we ought, but the Spirit Himself makes intercession for us with groanings which cannot be uttered. Now He who searches the hearts knows what the mind of the Spirit is, because He makes intercession for the saints according to the will of God." Romans 8:26-27

You are not smart enough to know how to pray the perfect will of God for yourself or anyone else. For we only know in part the mystery and will of God. Yet, Holy Spirit knows the perfect will of God and knows exactly how to pray for us. He even knows the things that our eyes have not seen, nor ears have heard, nor has even entered our imaginations what God has prepared for all of us who love God (1 Corinthians 2:9-12).

Receive this revelation today. Get to know the Holy Spirit. He is the executor of the New Testament Will of Jesus Christ. Talk to Him continuously. He is your Teacher, Counselor, Comforter, Spiritual Guide, and Memory Activator (John 14:1518,26). Ask Him to pray through you aloud the perfect will of God (Jude 20-21). Beseech Him to show you the things that God has freely given you. Entreat Holy Spirit to teach you.

"The Spirit of truth has come... He will tell you of things to come. He will glorify Me, for He will take of what is Mine and declare it to you. All things that the Father has are Mine. Therefore, I said that He will take of Mine and declare it to you." John 16:13-15

Faith Action Step

Yield to Holy Spirit. Allow Him to fill and lead you.

AFTERWORD

This ninety-day journey of building your faith and spirit on the Word of God is just an appetizer. To know Christ completely and receive all the promises of God you will need to immerse yourself in the Word of God daily to become intimately acquainted with Him. You will also need to rely on the Holy Spirit. Every day, implore Him to fill you with His power to love, live, serve, and share like Jesus. Read the New Testament Gospels of Christ frequently especially the Gospel of John. The gospels portray the life of Christ.

In them, Jesus talks and demonstrates to us how to live to please God, the Father. He shows us how to allow Heavenly Father to do the supernatural works of God through us. Throughout the day, continually, listen to praise and worship music, sermons on faith in the Word of God, and miraculous testimonies of God's faithfulness and healing. These spiritual activities will strengthen your faith and improve your entire health (brain, body, soul, and spirit).

The more you worship and fellowship with God, the more you will crave His presence. Feed your faith. Starve your doubts. Become addicted to God and His Word. You will lack nothing. His Spirit will overflow in you and fill you with the glory of God. Grace and peace be multiplied to you. Believe and receive the fullness of His power.

"For the kingdom of God is not in word but in power."
1 Corinthians 4:20

*"But you shall receive power when
the Holy Spirit has come upon you."*
Acts 1:8

FAITH TALK: WORD OF GOD SPEAK

TOPICAL INDEX

ABOUT THE AUTHOR

V onda Chipman is a dynamic practical Bible teacher and Pastoral counselor. Her transformative teaching and counseling ministries have helped thousands of people to experience lifelong spiritual growth and psychological and physical healing. She travels extensively teaching in churches and conferences throughout the year and ministering to people in various countries. She and her husband, Dr. Paul Chipman, have been married for over 34 years and in pastoral ministry for 30 years. They have three adult married sons and six grandchildren. For requests for her to minister at your church or conference or for further information for counseling, please visit the website: www.hopeforthehometoday.com or email her at www.info@hopeforthehometoday.com.

Made in the USA
Middletown, DE
26 June 2019